RUTH

LESSONS FROM THE BIBLE

NILANJANA DAS BARMAN

To the God who Saves

Contents

Preface

Coming from a Non-Christian background I have always felt inadequate in church. I do not know how to pray right or how to praise God in everything even when my heart acknowledges it. I am the last to provide witness during testimony time. That does not mean that God has done any less for me or that he does any less for me than for anyone else.

My feelings of inadequacy brought me to the story of Ruth. Born a Moabite and having been brought up in their culture I wonder how she settled in among her husband's people. She abandoned not just her home, her familiar surrounding but also her faith and her practices. She had only one tool in all that she did and that was obedience to her mother-in-law, Naomi.

In this study, I wish to focus on the relationship between these two women and how the beliefs of one shaped the other. In our walk of faith we are often in need of a Naomi. Naomi did not choose to return to Israel because of her faith in God. In fact the only reason she returned was that she had no where else to go. She had lost her husband and her two sons. In short she was a person who had nothing left to lose. Naomi sets for us an example of carrying on despite the situations. She considered herself too old to remarry and have a family again. She was a sojourner in a foreign land in a time of famine. In the patriarchal world of the time a woman without a male figure in the family rarely had any way to survive. Her desolation is made complete in the understanding that she asks her people to change her name from Naomi to Mara which means bitter. Naomi was bitter but not lost.

In her situation, Ruth provided her a reason to carry on. Among her two daughters-in-law, Orpah and Ruth, the latter decided to accompany her lonely mother-in-law. There was no social obligation for her to stay with Naomi. She could return back to Moab and take another husband and start a family. According to Israeli custom, Ruth was supposed to marry within the family but Naomi had no other children or the hope of any other children. So she was free to marry whoever she wants. Ruth however did not choose to let Naomi return alone. Her journey into the pages of the Bible doesn't start with hope or faith. It starts with her sense of duty towards her mother-in-law and her compassion towards a fellow widow who has lost everything.

In this study of the Bible we will be discussing about the various aspects of their relationship. The Bible leaves breadcrumbs for us to follow into their lives and each trail of bread crumb leads us to a treasure chest of wisdom and knowledge.

ACKNOWLEDGEMENTS

I hereby acknowledge that I am nothing without Jesus. I died to the world over a decade ago and He brought me back to life and keeps me living to this very day. Without His wisdom I am simple, uneducated and uncouth. I thank Him for my every breath.

I hereby thank my life partner, a gift from Jesus, who directs me back to my Lord and Master, whenerver my feet stray. He is a loyal shepherd appointed by the Good Sphepherd to keep His flock in check and I hope that my Lord empowers me to support him in every mortal way that I can.

I thank all those who have stood with me in my walk of faith. I also thank those who have stood against me, which has only strengthened my conviction in my God.

I thank my parents who have supported me despite the illusion that they believe to be their gods. I pray that God leads them to the truth.

Ultimately I thank the reader in showing interest in my walk of faith.

Prologue

Written in the times of the prophet Samuel, the story of Ruth adheres to the timeline of the early part of the book of Judges and as such is often times associated with it. The events pertaining to Ruth were believed to have taken place between 1160 B.C and 1100 B.C.

As to the author of this book, some attribute it to Eli the priest, who seems to have been too soon to give an account of the birth of David; others to Gad or Nathan; some to Hezekiah, and others to Ezra; but what the Talmudists assert, which is most generally received, and most probable, is, that it was written by Samuel; so they say Samuel wrote his own books, Judges, and Ruth; and it is commonly said that this book is an appendix to that of the Judges, and the introduction to 1 Samuel, and is fitly placed between them both. There are even claims that the book may have been written by Mordecai, the author and a chief character in the book of Esther.

Apart from Esther, Ruth is the only other book in the Bible named after a woman. Also, Ruth is the only book in the Bible where the protagonist of the story is the woman after whom the book is named. C. I Scofield in his commentary identifies the journey of Ruth with that of a Christian believer. Ruth also gives a normal Christian experience:

1. Ruth deciding, (Ruth 1)- The entire length of the narrative hinges on Ruth's decision to not remain in Moab but to follow Naomi into the land of her deceased husband.
2. Ruth serving, (Ruth 2)- Ruth serves Naomi without the

hope of any reward. She goes into the field collecting grain and making flour. She takes responsibilities she is not supposed to take, simply to comfort the woman who has lost enough.

3. Ruth resting, (Ruth 3)- Once Ruth finds the field of Boaz she finds help and some semblance of security among his women and servants. She receives help.
4. Ruth rewarded, (Ruth 4)- Ruth regains a husband, has a child and attains a legacy in the fact that she becomes the great-grandmother of the second king of Israel.

The Book of Ruth is divided into four distinct settings.

- 1st setting: The country of Moab. 1:1-18
- 2nd setting: A field in Bethlehem. 1:19 - 2:23
- 3rd setting: A threshing floor in Bethlehem. 3:1-18
- 4th setting: The city of Behtlehem. 4:1-2

The journey is symbolic as it marks an inward journey into God's covenant. Moab is outside of Judah. The fields were generally outside the city. The threshing fields closer to the cities and then finally the city of Bethlehem.

Though the book covers a time period of almost 10 years it is not surprising to find that the major part of the book spans only a short period of time. The speed with which the latter part of the narrative progresses seems to highlight the force of God's breakthrough.

I

The Famine

In the very first verse of Ruth, we are introduced to the concept of a famine that occurred in the land.

> ***"Ruth 1:1 Now it came to pass in the days when the judges ruled, that there was a famine in the land. And a certain man of Bethlehem-Judah went to sojourn in the country of Moab, he, and his wife, and his two sons."***

The question that arises is this, who are the people that are suffering from this famine? These are the same people who were fed by God in the wilderness. These were the people who were promised a land of milk and honey as they were led out of Egypt and into Canaan. That land became their home, their Israel, their Bethlehem. And yet they became sojourners in Moab. Did that mean that God's promises were lies like the lies spoken by politicians before the elections that rarely if ever get fulfilled?

Truth is this, that land of Milk and Honey could not be realized because God's promises had not seen their completion. But what about the people who occupied the land of Canaan before the Israelites? If we remember the report of the twelve spies from The Book of Numbers we will recall that the land was overflowing with milk and honey before the Israelites stepped there. Those who dwelled there were the descendants of Anak, a Nephilim. So, the land itself was not cursed even when the inhabitants were not the chosen people. When Israelites stepped there suddenly they were facing severe famine. Then obvious question is that was the promised land holding promises only for the ungodly?

> "***Num 13:27 And they told him, and said, We came unto the land whither thou sentest us, and surely it floweth with milk and honey, and this is the fruit of it.***"

Elimelech and his family had to travel to Moab with his entire family to avoid death by starvation. These Moabites were the same people with whom God had asked not to have any relationships. This was the Moab, whose king Balaak had bribed the prophet Balaam to curse the Israelites (Numbers 22-24). Despite the long-standing animosity between the people this family had chosen to sojourn in Moab. It was not a temporary situation either for their sons had married Moabite women. If they had the assurance that they would return to Judah, neither one of them would take a non-Israeli for a wife. Thus we see that the famine lasted a while and it was followed by personal loss.

Elimelech died. Naomi, the widow, was left in a foreign land with two sons. That is when they took Moabite wives. It can be easily imagined that Naomi was cut off from her kin and kind. She was trying to find bearing in a foreign land but even that was taken away from her when not one, but both sons passed away.

A famine refers to a shortage. It is not necessarily a shortage of food. Wikipedia defines, "A famine (as) a widespread scarcity of food, caused by several factors including war, inflation, crop failure, population imbalance, or government policies. This phenomenon is usually accompanied or followed by regional malnutrition, starvation, epidemic, and increased mortality." Elimelech had escaped from Bethlehem to flee from this increased death and that resulted in the wiping out of the family line with no male heir remaining. Elimelech may have faced material famine in Bethlehem but Naomi faced social and spiritual famine in Moab.

Naomi faced a shortage of a reason to struggle in a foreign land. She faced a shortage of social relevence in the absence of a male member of the family. That was accompanied by material shortage as well as women were not the socially accepted earning members of the family. In the mean time the famine in her own country had been resolved by divine intervention. That is when she decided to return to Bethlehem irrespective of whether she would be accepted or not. Her moral famine was too severe to care for the social situation of a widow in Israel. Nonetheless, she wished well for her daughters-in-law.

If we are to go by example, Naomi could have treated her daughters-in-law severely. Judah had assumed Tamar to be the cause of his sons' deaths and had condemned her to a solitary life. Naomi did not do that. She did not blame her daughters for the deaths of her sons. What she did was she wished them well and asked them to live even when she was not looking forward to life herself. This is the reason every outsider needs a Naomi in their walk of faith- to push them forward despite their reluctance to move.

This brings us back to the concept of Famine. Elimelech and Naomi left for Moab not because they were going hungry in Bethlehem but because the produce of the land was unable to meet their hunger. That is true for many of us today. We go through periods of crisis because we fail to appreciate the stock available to us. When Naomi returns to Bethlehem we find that she had indeed realized where the true famine lay.

> ***"Ruth 1:21 I went out full, and the LORD hath brought me home again empty: why then call ye me Naomi, seeing the LORD hath testified against me, and the Almighty hath afflicted me?"***

If only we too could realize in time that where our famine or the starvation truly comes from. The starvation was more spiritual than physical. It was not exclusive to Elimelech and Naomi but rather something prevalent in the land at that time. People failed to recognize that the source of this could be a separation from God. Nowhere in the entire book of Ruth do we find any prayer or any act of God. The pious greetings among the people seem a form of lips service at most, the kind that Jesus warns us against. Could that be the source of the starvation?

When we hear of starvation in the Bible, in Genesis God led Joseph to prepare for the famine in Egypt. That famine had a purpose. It firmly established Joseph as the second-in-command to the Pharoah and it provided the sojourning Israel a place to anchor and multiply. That starvation led to a four hundred years settlement in the land of Egypt. Yes, there was slavery faced in the land and there were the ten plagues but seventy turned into thousands in Egypt. So the famine in Egypt led to the growth of God's people. So it is only expected that a famine in Israel leads to some other form of growth. That growth is seen in the form of Ruth. The inclusion of a foreigner amidst the chosen family of Israel is a foreshadowing of greater things to come. Ruth chose to be part of Israel, she chose to be a widower and a sojourner.

> "*Famine is an involuntary period of starvation while fasting is voluntary.*"

Israel was going through a period of starvation in the absence of God. The story of Ruth takes place in the time of the Judges. We know that the Judges were a period of disobedience, chastisement, and breakthrough of God. The famine, the spiritual famine of the people can be seen as the disobedience of the people as they fail to keep God at the centre of their lives. The tragedy that Naomi suffered can be seen as chastisement. The question that remains is that, where is the breakthrough?

For an aged widow like Naomi, the fact that her daughter-in-law does not abandon her to seek her future amidst her kinsmen is a breakthrough of sorts. All throughout the next part of the story we see that it is Ruth gathering food or seeking redemption from Elimelech's kinsman-redeemer. Ruth assumes the duties that Naomi was incapable of performing due to her mourning, bitterness, and depression.

Naomi's emptiness in life was involuntary but Ruth's was not. Ruth chose this life of her own free will out of her loyalty to a husband who was not living and for a family that could not provide her with any security. While Naomi faced famine, Ruth underwent fasting. The breakthrough in Ruth's life came through the presence of the Kinsman-redeemer in the form of Boaz. That was the blessing at the end of her fast rather than a breakthrough at the end of a chastisement.

II

The Harvest

Naomi did not return to Bethlehem because she had nothing to live for in Moab. She returned home when she found out that the Israelites were no longer suffering from the famine. Naomi was chasing ways to absolve her physical hunger. At times her spiritual immaturity contrasts with the loyalty and steadfastness shown by her Moabite daughter-in-law. Naomi grew up among stories of the wonderful deeds of the Lord. However the way she and her family lived their life seems to be fickle in contrast to Ruth's steadfast devotion.

> ***"Ruth 1:6 Then she arose with her daughters in law, that she might return from the country of Moab: for she had heard in the country of Moab how that the LORD had visited his people in giving them bread."***

When Ruth and Naomi came to Bethlehem it was the time for the Barley harvest. It is important to notice that they are returning to the land that Naomi left because of famine only to lose several important things in their lives and come back to find a harvest.

Let us list some of the losses that Naomi suffered in Moab:

1. She lost her national identity as an Israelite. She was a sojourner, a refugee in the land. As a result she was deprived of the pride of being the chosen people of God.
2. She lost her home. The tribes of Israel were all given an inheritance in the land of Canaan which was to be their home. Naomi's home was Bethlehem. When she left the land she lost her true home.
3. Naomi lost her husband. When Elimelech died in Moab, Naomi wasn't only widowed. She was left without a guardian. She had no kinsman redeemer and in the patriarchal home, her immediate guardians became her two sons.
4. Naomi lost her sons Mahlon and Chilion. In a land obsessed with offsprings and inheritance Naomi became childless with no hope of future children at her age, especially without a husband.

However for Ruth it is different. On coming to Israel Ruth stands to lose a lot many things. Remember that this is the land where bloodline is very important and someone not born of Abraham is seen as a second class citizen in the least. Their own law states that such a family would not be deemed pure for ten generation. Ruth knew that she would be treated with contempt in Israel, if not from all then from some. She was mentally prepared for that.

Ruth, who we learn was quite a young woman did not stand much chance of a home and a family in Israel. No one was likely to want a foregner and a widow for a wife, knowing that her first born would bear the name of her dead husband. If she remained in Moab, among her people, she had a better chance of securing a husband and a home. That is what Naomi was pushing her towards. That is what Orpah settled for.

Ruth was a Moabite, married in the land of Moab. It is not fantastic to assume that she was surrounded by her kinsman and family from her father's side. That was not so in Israel. The only one she would have in Israel was a bitter and mourning mother-in-law.

As two widows, the chances of Naomi and Ruth being well fed or well off is impossible in the patriarchal world of ancient Israel where women are parcelled off with a piece of land. Ruth did not even have any hope of material comfort even when there seemed to be food in Israel. Without an earning member whatever Ruth could earn was through the grace and favour of those around her.

Ruth had more reasons not to go to Bethlehem than Naomi had to go to Moab. The one thing that kept her going was her loyalty to her deceased husband and his family. Mahlon is not mentioned many times in the book but his presence is a guiding factor to the narrative. We know little about him except his family but we know that his widow makes a vow to his family after his death that is till this day regarded as a wedding vow.

> ***"Ruth 1:16-17 And Ruth said, Intreat me not to leave thee, or to return from following after thee: for whither thou goest, I will go; and where thou lodgest, I will lodge: thy people shall be my people, and thy God my God: Where thou diest, will I die, and there will I be buried: the LORD do so to me, and more also, if ought but death part thee and***

> ***me.*"**

When Ruth arrived it is the time of the harvest and in that she finds food by gleaning the ears of corn that are left behind after reaping. It was a custom of the Israelite to not go back for the ears that was missed during harvest to feed the widow and the travellers. Ruth was both.

> "***Lev 23:22 And when ye reap the harvest of your land, thou shalt not make clean riddance of the corners of thy field when thou reapest, neither shalt thou gather any gleaning of thy harvest: thou shalt leave them unto the poor, and to the stranger: I am the LORD your God.***"

We see that when Naomi chose to walk out of God's covenant, in search of food, she lost everything. When Ruth decided to walk in the covenant of God, though the covenant was not hers to claim, by marriage she took part in the promise of God.

Though the book of Ruth talks about widowhood a lot, the book is mostly about marriage. The harvest is an important symbolism in that context as marriage is inexplicably linked with fertility and furthering the family line. Ruth was faithful in her marriage which was short lived. The God of second chances, therefore offered her a second chance at marriage.

III

The Bitterness

When Naomi returned to Bethlehem she asked others to call her ***Mara*** which means bitter. She was bitter with life. She was old and without any hope of remarriage. She had lost both her children to death and had nothing to live for except for a stubborn daughter-in-law who refused to leave her alone. We do not know what prompted Ruth to accompany Naomi to Bethlehem. It is definitely a testament to her loyalty to her wedding vows. Nonetheless, a major guiding factor that may have led to her actions could be Naomi's desolation.

Naomi's life gives us several pointers as to how not to deal with our grief.

- The first thing that Naomi did was that she turned her grief into a label. When she calls herself Mara, she is turning her mourning into her identity. Often times we get so used to being miserable that it becomes a lifestyle rather than a situation. The same was happening with Naomi. Grief does not mean that we become negligent of our duties and responsibilities. We need to understand grief as a part of our lives and overcome it through hope, faith and perseverence. Naomi did not believe that her life could ever become better again. She was bitter to the point where she refused hope and faith.

- Naomi focussed on her loss as the only prominent thing in her life. She idolised her loss in a sense and refused to acknowledge any of the good things happening in her life beyond it. Naomi failed to focus on the fact that the famine which drove them out of Israel was over. Naomi failed to register that she had gained a daughter in Moab, a daughter whom she had not birthed. We need to always keep our focus on the blessings of God, more in times of adversity than in prosperity. In times of prosperity it is easy to label ourselves blessed but during adversity it is those blessings that give us the strength to carry on.
- Naomi abandoned Ruth when she was in need of introduction to those in whose eyes she could find favour. The fact that she ended up in the field owned by Boaz is a coincidence in itself which Naomi later acknowledges. Grief takes away our capacity to think and act. In Naomi's case it was nothing different. Naomi let her sense of responsibility towards her daughter slip away as she indulged herself in self-pity.

Ruth provides a contrast to Naomi in terms of strength and facing adversity. She too had lost her husband. She had left her family and kin. She was in a land of strangers. Her only companion was a bitter old woman. On the other hand Ruth was a young woman but she was wise beyond her years. She was humble enough to seek guidance from those elder to her and show obedience to their words of wisdom. At the same time she was also dilligent enough in her own work.

> "*Ruth 2:6-7: And the servant that was set over the reapers answered and said, It is the Moabitish damsel that came back with Naomi out of the country of Moab: And she said, I pray you, let me glean and gather after the reapers among the sheaves: so she came, and hath continued even from the morning until now, that she tarried a little in the house.*"

Ruth was hard working. She was also responsible. She had to take care of her mother-in-law who was not in a situation to help herself. Naomi was suffering from grief after suffering the loss that she faced in her life. We almost always hear about the five stages of grief that one experiences. We do not know whether Naomi went through each of them but the result of several of them are evident in her character.

1. **Denial, numbness, and shock**: Numbness is a common reaction to a death or loss. This stage of grief helps protect us from experiencing the intensity of the loss. As we move through the experience and slowly acknowledge its impact, the initial denial and disbelief fades. The story of Ruth does not mention how long Naomi suffered from the shock of losing her husband and her two young sons within such a short time. But it does mention that after a while she rose with her two daughters in law. That means for a while she must have been immobile, held in her place by numbness and shock.

2. **Bargaining**: This stage of grief may be marked by persistent thoughts about what "could have been done" to prevent the death or loss. If this stage of grief isn't dealt with and resolved, the person may live with intense feelings of guilt or anger that can interfere with the healing process. For Naomi this never became much of an issue as a woman in those times did not have ample responsibilities to shoulder in the presence of the men. That automatically translated to the fact that they could not carry guilt for something they did not have control over. Naomi did not have a say in the decision to move to Moab, nor in the decision to stay there. One output of this could have been Naomi blaming her daughters in law which she did not do. That tells us that Naomi was able to resolve this stage of grief.
3. **Depression**: In this stage, we begin to realize and feel the true extent of the death or loss. Common signs of depression in this stage include trouble sleeping, poor appetite, fatigue, lack of energy, and crying spells. We may also add self-pity and feel lonely, isolated, empty, lost, and anxious. This is the stage that we find Naomi in as she comes back to Bethlehem. When she returns to Israel, everything reminds her of the family that she had and then lost. Hence her feeling of emptiness and loss is magnified.
4. **Anger:** This stage is common. It usually happens when we feel helpless and powerless. Anger can stem from a feeling of abandonment because of a death or loss. Naomi could not afford to go through this stage because of the constant presence of Ruth. Ruth did not allow Naomi to feel helpless or powerless. She stood up beside her mother-in-law as her strength, comfort and support.

5. **Acceptance**: In time, we can come to terms with all the emotions and feelings we experienced when the death or loss happened. Healing can begin once the loss becomes integrated into our set of life experiences. Perhaps Naomi truly accepted her loss with the birth of Obed. Nonetheless she required the presence of Ruth to achieve it.

Naomi's grief kept her from accompanying her daughter-in-law while she gathered food. Her mind was too occupied with her loss to bother about Ruth's safety, the safety and precaution which Boaz had to take care of.

> "***Ruth 2:8-9: Then said Boaz unto Ruth, Hearest thou not, my daughter? Go not to glean in another field, neither go from hence, but abide here fast by my maidens: Let thine eyes be on the field that they do reap, and go thou after them: have I not charged the young men that they shall not touch thee? and when thou art athirst, go unto the vessels, and drink of that which the young men have drawn.***"

One could perhaps say that Naomi's actions towards Ruth was negligent. She had sent her young and widowed daughter in law, who is a stranger to the land, without protection or a chaperon, to collect food for the both of them. Yes it was Ruth who had sought her permission to do so. However as a mother figure Naomi should have thought about the only living member of her family. But she was too engrossed in her bitterness to give it a thought. Only when Ruth returned with news of their kinsman redeemer did Naomi show some positive action or attitude. The hope of her family line being restored was perhaps the trigger that could bring her out of her depression.

Depression does not come from God. We experience depression when we allow our earthly situation to overwhelm us and we ignore that there is a divine plan acting through every blessing and adversity. We are not privy to the complete plan of God but relying on Him for comfort and direction is the only way we can deal with adversity, loss and grief without it overpowering our sense of justice and purpose. Naomi saw her grief as a punishment from God. She failed to acknowledge however that God's ultimate work turns out for good.

> ***"Rom 8:28 And we know that all things work together for good to them that love God, to them who are the called according to his purpose."***

IV

The Foreigner

Let us focus for a while on Ruth. She is a Moabite woman. She is a foreigner and she is alone. Her mother-in-law is a depressed bitter woman who is busy counting her losses. She is so busy in her own sorrow that she fails to accompany her daughter-in-law in gathering grains or introducing her to family and kin. Ruth does it all alone. She works from morning to the late evening, only going to the house once perhaps to check on her mother-in-law. She gathers grains, roasts and grinds them, bringing the flour to her mother-in-law. She provides for her family in the place of her dead husband.

Ruth embodies the Proverb 31 woman long before the Book of Proverbs was composed. We do not know how Ruth carried out her household responsibilities while Mahlon was alive or when she was married to Boaz. The Book of Ruth only talks about her period of widowhood. There is no example of the life and responsibilities of a married woman in Israel given prior to the description of Ruth. The only mention of married women in the tribes is provided in the rules and laws of Moses. Ruth does not require to adhere to those laws being a Moabite.

> "***Pro 31:25 Strength and honour are her clothing; and she shall rejoice in time to come.***"

Ruth's choices are different from that of the women before her. Sarah followed her husband because she had nothing to live for in her own land. She was childless and menopausal. She was perhaps tired of the shame of being barren and chose to follow her husband into a land of promise. We see her failing to share her husband's trust and thrusting her maid onto him for childbearing. We see her unwonted jealousy as she mistreats her servant and later makes her leave the security of the tribe towards an imminent death in the wilderness. What we fail to recognize is that the child that Hagar carries with her is also Abraham's seed, though not the seed of promise nonetheless, his child and Sarah fail to treat the child of her husband with anything close to compassion.

Rebekkah tricks her husband into blessing her favourite son. That leads to a war between her sons and enmity between the two lands. Rebekkah takes advantage of her husband's blindness and fools him. Her success in doing so is also her failure in being a good wife and mother. She does injustice to one of her sons and her husband while trying to do well by Jacob.

Rachel steals her father's household idols despite knowing of her husband's faith. She not only insults her husband's faith but also desecrates the faith of her father by sitting on the idols and claiming to be unclean. A major portion of Rachel's life is spent in jealousy of the fact that her sister has had more children than her even when she enjoyed the undivided love and attention of her husband.

Rachel went on to barter her husband for a few mandrakes.

> ***"Gen 30:14-15 And Reuben went in the days of wheat harvest, and found mandrakes in the field, and brought them unto his mother Leah. Then Rachel said to Leah, Give me, I pray thee, of thy son's mandrakes. And she said unto her, Is it a small matter that thou hast taken my husband? and wouldest thou take away my son's mandrakes also? And Rachel said, Therefore he shall lie with thee to night for thy son's mandrakes."***

Later on, we read of Potiphar's wife who tried to seduce Joseph in the absence of her husband and though one may argue that she was not an Israelite, well, neither was Ruth. We read of Zipporah, a Cushite and though she took it upon herself to fulfil the covenant of circumcision to save the life of her husband, little else is said to reference her involvement in her husband's affairs. Moses having married her even becomes a point of conflict with Miriam who is later punished by God for her objections.

We read of Caleb's daughter but there is no description provided of her nature or her manners. A contrast is provided by Deborah, a Judge, who frees the people of an oppressor.

We read of Jephthah's daughter whom he unknowingly promised as a sacrifice and who abided by her father's wish. Though it reflects a heart of devotion it also shows helplessness that cannot be overlooked. The Law of Moses disregards the vows by wives if their husbands object. However, the life of a girl is vowed away by the father and nothing is done to prevent it. In truth, it is a lesson in both foolishness and superstition if it is to be believed that such a sacrifice is pleasing to the Lord for we know how He provided the ram for Abraham and His Son for all humanity. The daughter, though seeking time from her father to reconcile with her fate, fails to present reason to him and fails to uphold the fact that taking human life is a sin, to begin with.

Then there is Delilah, a Timnite, another foreigner. She betrays her husband time and time again and Samson chooses to trust her repeatedly till she leads him to blindness and death. These are mostly the examples of women we find before or around the time of Ruth. Also, we see the plight of women in Israel during the time of Judges in Judges 19-21. Though this perhaps occured after Ruth's time, it gives us an idea about the temperament of the people contemporary to Ruth. The mistreatment of the women and the wives is all explained in the last line of the book of Judges.

> ***"Jdg 21:25 In those days there was no king in Israel: every man did that which was right in his own eyes."***

This brings us to the story of Ruth. The story takes place in the time of the Judges. We do not hear of a King or a Judge. Yet we hear of a foreigner's faith in the people to whom she had married. Her faith does not stem from a place of helplessness like Jephthah's daughter. Her faith stems from her own strength and commitment to her deceased husband. She embraces the covenant of her husband's God, not out of Zipporah's desperation but out of respect for her family. She chooses her vows over her comfort, unlike Delilah. She does not choose her own greatness like Deborah but chooses to silently toil and support her lonely mother-in-law. There are so many lessons to learn from Ruth but one of the greatest lessons she succeeds to impart is that of selflessness.

V

The Sheaves

The sheaves are an important symbol in the study of the Book of Ruth. They are a promise to foreigners and widows that Ruth claims when Naomi fails to. They are also a symbol of blessings that arrive before us with a choice, whether to receive or not. The blessings arrived at the hands of Boaz, a kinsman, an extended family, not a stranger who could be mistaken for an angel, but rather a human being. God often acts through human beings rather than the supernatural. Yet Boaz's kindness reflects that mercy and genorosity of God proving that despite the Fall man does retain a semblance of the image of God, especially while acting within the will of God.

> ***"Ruth 2:15-16 And when she was risen up to glean, Boaz commanded his young men, saying, Let her glean even among the sheaves, and reproach her not: And let fall also some of the handfuls of purpose for her, and leave them, that she may glean them, and rebuke her not."***

Ruth had gained favour with Boaz, not through her action but through her reputation. Even before Boaz knew who she was, he had heard of her. When the servant told Boaz that Ruth was the Moabite who had accompanied Naomi, Boaz held a kind disposition towards her. He did not treat her as a foreigner but rather acknowledged her as kin and called her "daughter" due to her youth.

The report that Boaz had received of her was that of a hard-working woman. His earnest desire was to preserve the spirit of hard work in her. So he offered her a form of protection. Boaz went to the Moabite and specifically asked her to glean among his crops, stick close to his women and not go to other fields. He did not do so out of pity but out of the knowledge of men and how they could perceive a young widow in a foreign land.

That kind of attitude is not uncommon in today's day and time. Women, who are willing to push boundaries for personal or family ambitions are often taken advantage of in this world. Boaz recognised that amidst the men and society of his time. He did not have control over everyone. However, he had control over his own men and faith in his own authority and he exercised that authority to provide sanctuary to this woman.

He extended his trust towards her by allowing her to glean not just at the edge of the fields but also among the sheaves, the area where the grains were being bound into sheaves by young women and where anyone might have the best opportunity to steal from the bound sheaves if they so desired. Apart from the trust Boaz also showed generosity. That generosity is evident in his command to his young men to purposefully drop some of the crops so that Ruth may glean from them as well.

> ***"Ruth 2:20 And Naomi said unto her daughter in law, Blessed be he of the LORD, who hath not left off his kindness to the living and to the dead. And Naomi said unto her, The man is near of kin unto us, one of our next kinsmen."***

When Ruth returned to Naomi with the ephah (22 litres) of barley that she had got from the gathered grains, Naomi knew immediately that this couldn't have been obtained from leftover grains. Naomi immediately recognized the generosity that had multiplied Ruth's efforts. The generosity was not only done towards Ruth but also towards Naomi because returning from a foreign land they had been depleted of all resources. God's providence met them through Boaz's kindness.

The Sheaves represent that providence which was a precursor of greater things in life. Ruth being a foreigner did not understand that Boaz went out of his ways to help a foreigner. If she did perhaps she would not have taken so fondly to his kindness. In life we often refuse help from others when we feel that it is undue. However God often works undue favours upon us for the fulfilment of his purpose. The natural human reaction is to fight that favour. We want to be responsible for our own situation. When we pray fror supernatural intervention we want that to be some kind of miracle but we forget that God choses to perform miracles through the works of others. When we are hankering after our own personal miracle we are perhaps refusing a hundred of them coming our way.

The book of Ruth teaches us to accept the blessings that come from known sources. In order for the Kinsman redeemer to redeem he has to be closely related to the family. But what is more important than the blood connection is the connection. When Naomi shunned her people and travelled to Moab she did not have a hope of redemption. Naomi's redemption came through Ruth, her only connection.

Connections are important in life no matter what their nature be. When we refuse to reach out and connect with people, we are shutting out the Grace of God that He chooses to act through them. Half of the message of the cross is to love your neighbour, those around you, those that you are dealing with daily. In times of loss, it is natural to shut people out. But had Ruth chosen to do the same as her mother-in-law the only fate that would have awaited them was starvation. Instead, she brought an ephah of barley home. That is the difference between blocking God's blessings and allowing it.

VI

The Redemption

Redemption comes from God but through His instruments. Redemption from sin comes from Jesus but comes through the Gospel. That is the reason behind the Great Commission. The Gospel must be spread for the Redemption to be claimed.

The redemption sought by Ruth was not a spiritual redemption but rather a social one. Being a Moabite, married to an Israelite who died in Moab, Ruth's social relevance in Israel was limited. The redemption that she could avail, however, would not be solely for her, but also for her husband's family. Through her, there was a chance for Mahlon's name to live on.

> "***Deu 25:5-6 If brethren dwell together, and one of them die, and have no child, the wife of the dead shall not marry without unto a stranger: her husband's brother shall go in unto her, and take her to him to wife, and perform the duty of an husband's brother unto her. And it shall be, that the firstborn which she beareth shall succeed in the***

name of his brother which is dead, that his name be not put out of Israel."

Mahlon did not have a living brother to ensure that his name lived on. However, Boaz was one of the nearest relatives who could fulfil that purpose. Now it is up to Ruth to claim that redemption and for Boaz to provide it. Please note that this is the same Ruth who refused to stay back in Moab to find a husband and family among her own people. Whether it was due to her loyalty to her dead husband or her affection for her lonely mother-in-law, choosing to be redeemed by a man she barely knew made Ruth put power into a hand she couldn't fully trust. The question then arises that why did she do it.

Obedience-a way to Redemption:

Naomi instructed her in this matter. Ruth trusted Naomi and her judgement. Ruth knew Boaz to be a kind man, a man of authority among his servants. Was that truly enough of a reason to offer herself for marriage to him? Ruth's decision was never to go to Boaz for redemption but rather to obey her mother-in-law, her only immediate family.

Obedience plays a large part in God's plan for salvation. Our decision to obey God rather than our judgement often leads us closer to Him and His plans for us. Ruth had no way to know then that she would give birth to a line of Kings, nor could she imagine that she would be part of the family of the Saviour, the Son of God. At the critical moment, Ruth knew that God had given her the responsibility of bringing redemption to Naomi and her family by fueling the hope that Mahlon's name could live on through her offspring. In fact, it isn't Mahlon's name that we find in the genealogy of Jesus as much as we encounter the name of Ruth, a Moabite and a foreigner.

> "***Mat 1.5-6 And Sulmon begat Booz of Rachab; and Booz begat Obed of Ruth; and Obed begat Jesse; And Jesse begat David the king; and David the king begat Solomon of her that had been the wife of Urias;***"

In a manner, Ruth's social redemption is directly linked with our spiritual redemption. God's salvation plan was never meant to be exclusively for the Israelites. God called Abraham to be a blessing for all nations. Ruth is symbolic of that foreign element in God's salvation plan.

Redemption as a path rather than an outcome:

The manner in which Ruth's redemption was achieved is however questionable. Ruth did not wait for her kinsman-redeemer to claim her redemption. She approached Boaz, a reputable man, known for his kindness and generosity to act on her behalf even though he is not the closest relation to her husband and does not enjoy the privilege of being the first to claim rights to redeem her. Ruth and Naomi understood that redemption is not a miracle that you wait for. It is a path that you need to walk on.

Naomi prompted Ruth into action who then obeyed and that forced Boaz into action. Action is an important part of God's plan. Salvation does not come by only believing. It requires the component of acting on that faith by confessing and living a transformed life. It is true that faith is the seed of transformation but without that transformation, the faith is not substantiated.

> ***"Rom 10:9 That if thou shalt confess with thy mouth the Lord Jesus, and shalt believe in thine heart that God hath raised him from the dead, thou shalt be saved."***

Naomi, Ruth and Boaz all acted to accomplish the act of redemption and only then did they partake in the promise of God that was yet hidden from them.

Redemption: a blessing for all

True redemption is not a ticket to personal joy or pleasure. Redemption serves as healing to all parties concerned. God did not design the plan of redemption to benefit one party and not the other. When the law is laid in the Pentateuch where a brother redeems the name of his dead sibling by taking the wife and bearing a child who is to carry on the deceased sibling's name, all parties involved are being blessed. The deceased sibling has his name carried forth, the wife gets home, a family and security and the brother get a wife and offsprings.

In Ruth's case, redemption has a few more aspects to consider. As a result of redemption, Naomi received a son she did not have hope of gaining because of her age and social position. Ruth, a foreigner, received a place in the history of Israel as the great grandmother of the second King of Israel and an ancestor to the saviour. Boaz received a place in the genealogy of the Messiah. The Redemption plan of God proved to be inclusive of foreigners. It is proved that God's redemption plan is flexible enough to reach out to the rest of the world.

> ***"Ruth 4:13-14 So Boaz took Ruth, and she was his wife: and when he went in unto her, the LORD gave her conception, and she bare a son. And the women said unto Naomi, Blessed be the LORD, which hath not left thee this day without a kinsman, that his name may be famous in Israel."***

The ultimate purpose of God's redemption plan is to bring Him glory. If we are not working for the glory of God then we are not working within His redemption plans. His redemption plan requires action, sometimes immediate action under absolute obedience. To those who are capable of such, He grants abundant blessings, sometimes unforeseeable blessings. Ultimately we have to first choose to act according to His plan because that is the purpose of free will. Ruth followed Naomi to Israel of her free will and obeyed Naomi of her free will. She was ultimately blessed beyond her expectation.

We never find out whether Ruth found out within her lifetime about the abundant blessings that her lineage was heading towards. In fact, before Samuel visited Jesse there is no mention of any indication by God that Ruth's family will be the chosen Kings of Israel. Often we never know what greater blessings our salvation plan will lead to or who may be blessed by our obedience, our witness, or our confession. We need to walk by faith and know that God will use our actions for His glory as long as we abide by His will.

VII

The Kinsmen

The word kinsman refers to a male blood relative, one of the same family and ethnicity. Ruth had left all her kinsmen behind in Moab. Boaz was not her kinsman. Boaz was Naomi's kinsman. He was Elimelech's blood relative. But Naomi sent Ruth to Boaz to request him to redeem her.

> ***"Ruth 2:1 And Naomi had a kinsman of her husband's, a mighty man of wealth, of the family of Elimelech; and his name was Boaz."***

Naomi could have sought redemption from Boaz for herself. We know that though Naomi was much older than Ruth she was still capable of bearing children as it is Naomi who tells her daughters-in-law in Moab that she could not ask them to wait for her to find a husband and then have children who would grow up and marry them. But Naomi sent Ruth in her place to the threshing floor to request Boaz. It was unconventional. What Ruth lacked in her origin she made up for in her reputation and youth.

> ***"Ruth 3:10-11 And he said, Blessed be thou of the LORD, my daughter: for thou hast shewed more kindness in the latter end than at the beginning, inasmuch as thou followedst not young men, whether poor or rich. And now, my daughter, fear not; I will do to thee all that thou requirest: for all the city of my people doth know that thou art a virtuous woman."***

Boaz acknowledged Ruth's choice as a kindness. It is not difficult to imagine that Boaz was advanced in years. The authority he commanded over his servants spoke of experience. We do not find whether he had other wives or concubines though in the times of the Judges when the story unfolds, polygamy was not as rare. Nonetheless redeeming the widow of a kinsman was a duty bound to be performed in Israel. There are however two facts that were peculiar about this case:

- Boaz would be bound to marry Elimelech's widow, Naomi, by the rules of his people, not a daughter-in-law and a foreigner in that.
- Boaz wasn't the closest relative, bound to redeem this family. Still, he promised Ruth that he would do whatever was required to do right by Ruth.

> ***"Ruth 3:13-14 Remain tonight, and in the morning, if he will redeem you, good; let him do it. But if he is not willing to redeem you, then, as the LORD lives, I will redeem you. Lie down until the morning." So she lay at his feet until the morning, but arose before one could recognize another. And he said,***

"Let it not be known that the woman came to the threshing floor.""

Now, this other kinsman paints a contrast to Boaz in several ways. He was eager to step in and redeem any property that Naomi was willing to sell as long as it furthered his own inheritance. But he refused to allow the name of Elimelech or his sons to continue. As a result, he refused to take Ruth as his wife because the first child born would bear Mahlon's name and that child would claim the property redeemed from Naomi. Another factor that could have played a role in the kinsman's decision was the fact that Ruth was a Moabite and accepting her as a wife would discredit his social position.

Boaz was far more confident in his own inheritance and in his own position to not be threatened by the prospect of bringing forth Mahlon's descendent. It is a reflection of his character. From his earliest introduction which we receive in the beginning, Boaz comes off as a pious and kind man. Despite having an overseer in his fields he went out to greet and meet the workers in his fields, enquired of them individually, gave helpful warnings to Ruth for her safety, made provisions for her without her knowing and then accepted the role of her redeemer without giving a thought to her ethnicity. He did not waste time after promising Ruth to do whatever was in his power to help her in any way he could. He did not step over the rightful redeemer and went to him to give him the first opportunity to redeem and only when he refused did Boaz take up the mantle of the kinsman redeemer.

"***Ruth 4:9-10 Then Boaz said to the elders and all the people, "You are witnesses this day that I have***

> ***bought from the hand of Naomi all that belonged to Elimelech and all that belonged to Chilion and to Mahlon. Also Ruth the Moabite, the widow of Mahlon, I have bought to be my wife, to perpetuate the name of the dead in his inheritance, that the name of the dead may not be cut off from among his brothers and from the gate of his native place. You are witnesses this day."***

Boaz followed a chain of authority. He went to the elders and resolved the matter before them. He kept witnesses to his dealings so that the entire transaction would be transparent. He also preserves Ruth's honour by keeping from the people that it was Ruth who requested him for redemption and not Naomi, another oversight on the part of the mother figure. Boaz's discretion, his speedy action and his propriety in dealing with the entire situation allow us a glimpse into why he commanded the authority that he did among his servants and family.

Ruth's obedience and Boaz's prompt action lead to the conception of a child who is a true kinsman to Naomi. She regains a son in Obed, born of Boaz and Ruth. The birth of Obed brings glory to the God who had orchestrated the entire situation with Ruth coming to Israel, Ruth finding the field of Boaz, winning his favour, and him redeeming her for his wife. Through this Naomi's wound of being childless is healed.

Through this entire experience, the one entity that remains is the true kinsman to Naomi, or Ruth or Boaz, the God who had a plan and who worked to bring forth a greater redemption plan which was already centuries in the making. Though the Book of Ruth does not have any specific prayer or miracle that takes centre stage in the narrative the presence of God is felt in acts of kindness and obedience that are prevalent throughout the narrative.

Ruth steps into the covenant of God that Naomi had walked out of and then experienced His providence. Boaz lives a pious life filled with kindness and respect for those around him. God leads them together though Naomi gets to act as a matchmaker and gains a son in return, her kinsman who redeems her not from her poverty but from her misery, depression and self-pity.

VIII

The Mothers

The Book of Ruth centres on the concept of marriage vows. But another prevailing theme in the book is that of motherhood. Naomi, a mother of two sons is rendered childless in Moab. Her plight is somewhat alleviated by the presence of Ruth, a daughter through marriage. However, the complete relief arrives in the form of Obed, the child born to Ruth from Boaz, for the purpose of restoring the house of Elimelech. In truth, the redemption belongs to Naomi and not Ruth because Ruth, the foreigner was never in need of redemption. Mahlon's death opened before her the path to return to her own people in her own land. Ruth had nonetheless chosen her marriage vows to take care of the mother who did not birth her. With the birth of Obed, Ruth continued to be the wife of Boaz. The difference that occurred was in the life of Naomi who no longer remained childless.

> ***"Ruth 4:13 So Boaz took Ruth, and she was his wife: and when he went in unto her, the LORD gave***

> ***her conception, and she bare a son.***"

The book of Ruth recognizes that children are a gift from God. Naomi's barrenness is also identified as proof of God's chastisement pronounced against her. That statement is however one born of grief and not enlightenment. Naomi, whose name means pleasant, in the absence of her husband and sons, chooses to call herself Mara or bitter. She is not spiritually drawn to determining the cause of her punishment but is more focused on the aftermath of it.

> "***Ruth 1:21 I went away full, and the LORD has brought me back empty. Why call me Naomi, when the LORD has testified against me and the Almighty has brought calamity upon me?"***"

When back in her country Naomi refuses to initially reach out to her kinsmen in the hope of being redeemed. She acknowledges that she is too old to have a husband. The loss of a husband does not overwhelm her as much as the loss of her sons. Her daughters-in-law are a reminder to her of that loss and that is a primary reason that Naomi chooses to send them back to their people before making the journey towards Israel.

> "***Ruth 1:12-13 Turn again, my daughters, go your way; for I am too old to have a husband. If I should say, I have hope, if I should have a husband also tonight, and should also bear sons; Would ye tarry for them till they were grown? would ye stay for them from having husbands? nay, my daughters; for it grieveth me much for your sakes that the hand of the LORD is gone out against me.***"

Ruth and Naomi arrived in Israel at the time of the barley harvest and for the next three months (i.e. till the wheat harvest) Ruth acted as the provider to the family while Naomi mourned her loss. After three months, by the time that Ruth had won enough favour in the eyes of Boaz, Naomi allowed herself to hope for a redemption that may have not come otherwise to her. Naomi was incapable of bearing a child to carry forth Elimelech's name but Ruth was. Even when Boaz places the condition before the other kinsman regarding Naomi's property Ruth is mentioned in an association with the property being sold by Naomi. Ruth's future is inexplicably entangled with Naomi's and thus the child born to Ruth is in effect a child born to further Naomi's family.

> "***Ruth 4:17 And the women her neighbours gave it a name, saying, There is a son born to Naomi; and they called his name Obed: he is the father of Jesse, the father of David.***"

Naomi is not mentioned in the genealogy of Jesus. But Obed finds prominent mention. Naomi's motherhood found an outlet in Obed. That didn't need a justification by law or inheritance.

IX

The Blessing

Obed was born for the purpose of gaining Mahlon's inheritance. But he wasn't just an heir. He was the factor that reconciled the gentile heritage of Ruth with the promised staff of Judah.

> ***"Ruth 4:5 Then Boaz said, "The day you buy the field from the hand of Naomi, you also acquire Ruth the Moabite, the widow of the dead, in order to perpetuate the name of the dead in his inheritance.""***

The inheritance was not just of Elimelech and Mahlon but originated in Judah. Obed not only inherited the land from his ancestor but also the promise and the blessing. He inherited it and passed it on to David, in the short term and to Jesus in the long run. David would not have existed if Obed did not exist in this family line. From David started the two lines leading to Joseph and Mary the two parental figures in the life of Jesus, one bringing to flesh the God incarnate.

> ***"Gen 49:10 The scepter shall not depart from Judah, nor the ruler's staff from between his feet, until tribute comes to him; and to him shall be the obedience of the peoples."***

Jazmin

Claiming the Blessing

The blessing that Obed represented was not a blessing that Ruth earned. It was not remuneration for her devotion to her deceased husband and her family. But rather, it was a blessing passed down through her husband's side and intended for her people as well as every other people that existed. It was Abraham's covenant which Ruth entered through marriage and which provided hope to all, Jews and Gentiles.

> ***"Gen 22:17-18 I will surely bless you, and I will surely multiply your offspring as the stars of heaven and as the sand that is on the seashore. And your offspring shall possess the gate of his enemies, and in your offspring shall all the nations of the earth be blessed, because you have obeyed my voice.""***

Often in life conduits of a blessing become more significant than the blessing itself. Abraham was deemed the conduit of these blessings and the Jews placed significance in bloodlines and purities. Jesus defied all that in being born into the bloodline of the Moabite. Ruth is blessed with the blessing of Abraham in place of Mahlon. Is the blessing exclusive to Ruth? It is not. The blessing could have been

Orpah's as well but she did not seek it. Orpah did not choose to be part of the covenant. Therein comes the gift of free will. Ruth chose the covenant by following Naomi into a foreign land, by accepting that foreign land and the people as her own, through marriage, till death do them apart. That is the reason we find Ruth blessed, not because she earned the blessing but because she claimed it.

Stepping Up

Boaz too takes a significant place in the story. He is portrayed as the kinsman redeemer who stepped up when the nearest kin failed to take responsibility for Ruth. Stepping up is an important lesson that we learn from the Book of Ruth. Ruth stepped up to take care of Naomi when she was left all alone after a tragedy. Boaz stepped up to take Ruth's responsibility after he was personally requested by Ruth on the insistence of the same Naomi.

When Abraham was asked to offer his promised son as a sacrifice, Abraham stepped up in an act of obedience which was ultimately rewarded two folds. Abraham not only received a blessing for his offspring but God provided a ram for the offering, a substitute, foreshadowing the greatest substitution that was to take place on the Cross.

> ***"Gen 22:1 And it came to pass after these things, that God did tempt Abraham, and said unto him, Abraham: and he said, Behold, here I am."***

Often in life, we fail to step up to the occasion and fulfil our duty or responsibility. That is not what Christian living is supposed to be like. Jesus did not shy away from taking the burden of the cross for the sake of those who did not deserve God's forgiveness. Nonetheless, He did so as an act of mercy. In the Christian faith, the question is never if the other person is deserving or not but rather if you are willing to help the other person.

Accepting Grace

Naomi had abandoned her people and her kinsmen in pursuit of prosperity in a foreign land. She returned home, losing everything of value. She tried to turn away her daughters-in-law and when one followed her to her homeland, forsaking Moab, Naomi did not bother to introduce her among the people till three months pass by and the people of Israel become favourable towards Ruth because of her dedication and hard work. Naomi doesn't play an active role in the story at all. But she is the focus of Ruth's mission to migrate to Judah. Naomi returns to Israel but fails to connect with her former family. Yet it is those people and Kinsman that provide her with an heir, even though that heir is conceived through Ruth, the Moabite.

Naomi places her daughter-in-law in the barn with Boaz in order to tempt him and in order to secure a marriage with him. Boaz refuses to yield to temptation and yet he accepts Ruth's request and does his best to redeem her and her family. They are rewarded with an heir, an heir that Naomi gets to call her son because he is born as heir to Mahlon. Did Naomi deserve that reward? That is not a question for us to answer. The fact is that Naomi did receive it as grace.

Finding Blessings

Oftentimes in life blessings fall our way. Our decision to claim it or not directs the path which our life will take. Sometimes we claim those blessings under the misguided notion that they are rewards due to us for an action we give ourselves credit for. At other times we refuse to claim a blessing for the fear that our compliance with them may seem as foolish or even immature. The truth is that blessings cannot be justified with logic or probability. A miracle is too hard a word for them. Miracles are blessings that occur despite the situation. But the God of the Universe does not need to always defy the rules of nature to act in our favour.

Are we confident enough in our faith to claim our blessings in the most impossible of situations? We do not need confidence in our own actions but only in the power of the God we serve. Once we claim the blessing we need to extend it because we serve a God who blesses us to be a blessing to others, not to horde His promises for our own benefit.

Are we proactive enough to step up and extend our blessing to those in need around us? Ruth was not blessed because of her actions but her actions stemmed from the fact that she was blessed to be part of Abraham's covenant and had claimed the blessing by choosing her marriage over her people. Do our actions proclaim how blessed we are?

X

The Lessons

Lesson 1- Contentment

The famine that Naomi experienced both in Israel and in Moab stemmed from the family's moral depravation. They failed to accept and appreciate God's providence and went looking for an abundance that could satisfy their greed and not just their need. Ruth on the other hand chose to be content with her lot, accepted her widowhood and followed her mother-in-law into a foreign nation. She was praised for her actions.

> ***"Mat 6:31-32 Therefore take no thought, saying, What shall we eat? or, What shall we drink? or, Wherewithal shall we be clothed? (For after all these things do the Gentiles seek:) for your heavenly Father knoweth that ye have need of all these things."***

Jesus tells us to be content in our lot because God knows what we need and provides for them accordingly. That does not mean we do not go through famine, whether it be physical or moral. Every one faces crisis situations but relying on God can get us through it. We do not need to rely on anything or anyone else. Contentment comes from knowing the God we serve, not what He has done and may do.

Lesson 2- Priorities

Naomi prioritized the physical and financial well-being of her family and followed them into Moab. Ruth prioritized the emotional and social well-being of her family and chose to support her mother-in-law by following her to a foreign land where she had the likelihood of being treated like a second-class citizen. However, Ruth knew that Naomi would be comforted there and thus chose to cut off all ties with her own people so that Naomi could have emotional and social support.

> ***"Mat 6:33 But seek ye first the kingdom of God, and his righteousness; and all these things shall be added unto you."***

Our priorities determine our spiritual well-being. Jesus asks us to seek first the Kingdom of God and the righteousness of God, not our material needs. This Kingdom, as Jesus further explains is established through two relationships-that with God, our maker and also with our neighbour, our fellow human beings. Ruth prioritised her relationships and her wedding vows over her personal well-being. Priorities are what allow us to choose God long after He has already chosen us.

Lesson 3- Acceptance

Depression is often a chronic condition. Sometimes the source of depression is circumstantial, sometimes physiological. In Naomi's case, the depression was circumstantial. She had suffered tremendous loss in a foreign land where she had no emotional or social support. She had to overcome the condition through acceptance of God's greater plan in her life. The process started with the realization of the existence of the kinsman redeemer. Naomi went from calling herself Mara to accepting Obed as the child whom she did not bear.

> ***"Rom 14:8 For whether we live, we live unto the Lord; and whether we die, we die unto the Lord: whether we live therefore, or die, we are the Lord's."***

Death is always difficult to accept but living in God's will is a conditioned response. The human flesh does not wish to understand or conform to the dynamics of the spirit world. As far as the material world is concerned, science informs us that 95% of our physical universe is unknown to us in the form of dark matter and dark energy. If that be the case, then how can we even attempt to understand the spiritual realm which lies beyond human senses? We learn to accept God's will through faith and only by faith.

Lesson 4- Selflessness

Ruth served her husband's family with utter selflessness. She did not choose her own prosperity but rather chose the welfare of her aged mother-in-law. She did not choose to have a family of her own but accepted a husband in Boaz, a man much older than her, a kinsman of her father-in-law so that the name of her husband could be carried forward. She toiled ceaselessly and obeyed without question. She paints a picture of submissive virtue that is difficult to portray but easy to admire.

> ***"1Th 5:15 See that none render evil for evil unto any man; but ever follow that which is good, both among yourselves, and to all men."***

It is easier to be selfless when it is a required code of conduct for Christian living. But that too comes with its own peril. The moment we desire to be selfless to be called selfless, some vested interest develops. Then the act no longer remains selfless. Luckily it is human nature to render evil for evil and therefore we need to be on a constant watch so that we end up doing good, not for our own interest but for the well being of others.

Lesson 5- Connections

Naomi returned to Bethlehem because she had no one in Moab. Ruth came to Bethlehem because she had Naomi there. Naomi was her one connection in Judah but that did not stop Ruth from forming new connections. She approached the women working in the fields and made introductions. She developed a good reputation for herself through the witness of people she had just met. That gave her a recommendation before Boaz who approached her with words of advice and assurance. Ruth formed connections that gave Naomi hope and that led to the family's redemption.

> ***"Gal 6:2 Bear ye one another's burdens, and so fulfil the law of Christ."***

Ruth chose to bear Naomi's burden. Boaz chose to lighten Ruth's burden. But the help was not a one time thing. Ruth was a constant companion to Naomi and Boaz was a constant assurance to both the widows. Connections are not a one time thing. We need to not only build connections but strenthen them through communication. Jesus did not say that whenever you are in trouble reach out to others. St. Paul askes us to bear each other's burden. Search for those who need help so that when it is your turn to ask for help you have allies on your side. Nurture connections till they turn into relationships that honour God.

Lesson 6- Obedience

Ruth obeyed her marriage vows. She obeyed Boaz's instructions. She followed her mother-in-law's advice. She lived within the covenant of her husband's people. Ruth shows obedience in numerous ways and there is no mention of any outward reward that she receives for it. Often we are taught obedience as an action deserving of a reward. Ruth practices obedience as a virtue. However such obedience needs to come with an allied gift-discernment. We should be clear about what to obey and what not to obey. Otherwise, obedience can become a vice.

> ***"John 15:10-11 If ye keep my commandments, ye shall abide in my love; even as I have kept my Father's commandments, and abide in his love. These things have I spoken unto you, that my joy might remain in you, and that your joy might be full."***

Obedience to the word of God brings joy in our life. It is the opposite of sorrow or regret. When obeying God's word we do not need to rely on our own discernment. That is an assurance we need to strive for.

Conclusion

From the point of view of modern society where divorce is so common the book of Ruth paints a picture of marriage that is difficult to associate with. Ruth stands by her wedding vows long after her husband is no more. She chooses her husband's side of the family over her own people, her own culture. She shows two features- submission and selflessness- that are often considered weak in a modern woman. Yet reading from the perspective of a Christian believer rather than a woman it is easily understood why the message of Ruth is important.

The message of the New Testament is rooted in submission to the will of God. Jesus, Himself submits to the will of God in the Garden of Gethsamane, setting for us an example to live by His will and not our own. Ruth exemplifies a similar attitude towards the people around her. She submits to God's will in accepting her widowhood and submits to the authority of her mother-in-law. Such submission is not easy and the Book of Ruth shows Naomi's struggle with accepting the fate that had been rendered upon her. Ultimately even Naomi accepted it all and moved on. She learned to love again when she received a son in Obed. Did that erase the pain of losing her husband and two sons? No, definitely not. What it did, however, was that it taught Naomi to live within the will of God.

Another side to Ruth is her selflessness. She could have chosen to be in Moab. She was young and could have found herself a husband, have a family and live among her people, within the culture she grew up in. Ruth however chose to forsake everything familiar to her, with little to no hope for a future, in a nation that did not look kindly upon foreigners. She was not thinking about herself. She was thinking about vows she made to a husband who was no more. She was thinking about an elderly mother-in-law who had lost her entire family. Oftentimes in the modern world, such sentiments are exploited. If Ruth were to exist in today's world she may as well have ended up as a servant to Naomi's relatives rather than as the wife of Boaz and the great-grandmother of King David. The reason is simple. People who care more about others than about themselves are taken advantage of. That is why the world teaches us to know when to put our foot down and learn to say no at one point. Jesus does not give us any similar instruction. He asks us to offer our shirt to the one who asks for our cloak. In short we, as Christians, are asked to go out of our way to help others, despite the consequences.

Ruth sets an example of virtue that does not stem from upbringing. She is a Moabite brought into Israel by marriage. That is a hope for a new believer coming from a family that does not know Christ. If Ruth, the Moabite, can find place in the genealogy of Jesus, then a new believer too, can find place, in the body of Christ, through the redeeming blood of Jesus.

Printed by Libri Plureos GmbH in Hamburg, Germany

9 798887 838168